Let's go to

MEXICO

Keith Lye

General Editor

Henry Pluckrose

Franklin Watts

London   New York   Sydney   Toronto

Words about Mexico

Acapulco
Amecameca
Aztec

bullfight

canyon
Caribbean
cemetery
centavo

Diego Rivera

earthenware

feast-days
fiestas

Guadalajara
Guadalupe

Ixtacihuatl

maize
missionaries
Mixtec
Monte Alban
Monterrey

Oaxaca

patron Saint
peninsula
peso
plantations

Popocatépetl
pyramid

Rio Grande

shrines
Sierra Madre
sombreros

Teotihuacán
Tijuana
tortillas

Yucatán

Zapotec
Zócalo

Franklin Watts Limited
8 Cork Street
London W1

ISBN UK edition: 0 85166 963 8
ISBN US edition: 0 531 04471 8
Library of Congress Catalog Card No:
82–50061

© Franklin Watts Limited 1982

Typeset by Ace Filmsetting Ltd.,
Frome, Somerset
Printed in Great Britain by
E. T. Heron, Essex and London

Maps: Tony Payne
Design and Editorial Services:
Grub Street
Photographs: Zefa; D. Turner, 8.

Mexico is a country in Latin America, and much of it is mountainous. These are the Sierra Madre Mountains. Mexico was the home of many Indian civilizations.

Monte Alban was a holy city built about 2,500 years ago by Zapotec Indians. It is in southern Mexico. Mixtec Indians conquered Monte Alban about 1,000 years ago. They made it into a cemetery.

   This mural in the National
Palace is painted by Diego Rivera
and is his vision of the Indian world
in Mexico. Through his paintings the
magnificent history of Mexico can be
understood.

Mexico City is the capital of Mexico. It stands on a high tableland called the Valley of Mexico. It is one of the world's largest cities with a population of about 10 million. It stands on the ruins of an ancient Indian city.

Mexico City contains a large central square called the Zócalo. On the far side of the square is the National Palace, the home of the president. This was first built for the Spaniard Hernando Cortés who between 1519 and 1521 conquered the Indian Aztec Empire.

Mexico City has many open-air restaurants. The cook is making tortillas. These are flat pancakes usually made from maize meal. Tortillas are eaten instead of bread. They are stuffed with spicy fillings.

The Latin American Tower is the
tallest building in Mexico. Because
it has foundation chambers which
float it will not be affected by
earthquakes which sometimes
occur in Mexico.

This picture shows some Mexican stamps and money. The units of money are the peso and centavo. There are 100 centavos in a peso.

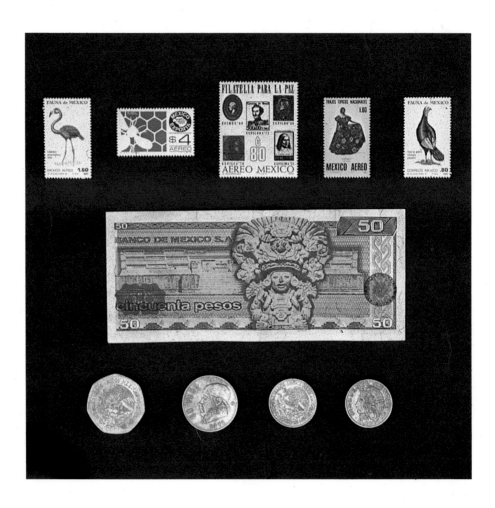

WORLD MAP

Mexico

UNITED STATES

Colorado

Rio Grande

Ciudad
Juárez

Bravo del Norte

Sierra

Chihuahua

Culiacan

Madre

Nuevo • Laredo

Torreón

Monterrey

*GULF OF
MEXICO*

MEXICO

Mazatlán

Tampico

Guadalajara

*PACIFIC
OCEAN*

Mexico City

Veracruz

Balsas

Acapulco

GUATEMALA BELIZE

11

The snow-capped volcano, Popocatépetl, is near Mexico City. Its name means "The Smoking Mountain". It is a dormant (sleeping) volcano.

The Rio Grande is a long river that forms part of Mexico's border with the United States. Mexico once owned large areas north of this river, including Texas. These were lost in a war with the United States (1846–48).

Maize, or corn-on-the-cob, is laid
out to dry on this farm near the
seaside resort of Acapulco. Maize is
Mexico's chief food crop. It is well
suited to the warm climate and
grows on more than half the country's
cultivated land.

14

Sugar cane is an important crop in hot and humid areas. The leading plantations are on the coastal plain bordering the Gulf of Mexico. Mexico is the world's fourth largest producer of cane sugar. It also produces bananas, cocoa, coffee, cotton and maize.

Coffee beans are loaded into tanks where they are washed and where their red skins are removed. Coffee grows well on southern mountain slopes. It is one of the main exports.

Red earthenware pots and vegetables are on sale at this busy market at Amecameca, a town near Mexico City. Many men wear hats with broad brims to keep the sun out of their eyes. Mexican sombreros have even larger brims.

Mexico is rich in minerals. This is a silver mine north of Mexico City. Mining and manufacturing employ fewer people than farming. But they provide more than three times as much money for Mexico as farming.

The most valuable mineral in Mexico today is oil. This oil rig is in the Gulf of Mexico, which borders the country in the north-east. In the whole of North and South America, only the United States and Venezuela produce more oil than Mexico.

Mexicans believe that education is extremely important. Education for children between 6 and 14 years of age is compulsory. But some areas, especially farming districts, do not have enough schools or teachers; so not all children can attend school.

The National University in
Mexico City has over 100,000
students. The university is the oldest
on the American continent and was
founded by Charles V of Spain in
1551. Mexico became independent
from Spain in 1821.

Many Mexicans in farm areas are poor. They live in wooden huts with earth floors. But they dress up when their pictures are taken. Of every 100 people in Mexico, 55 are of mixed race (Indians and Spaniards), 29 are Indian and 15 are European.

These girls in Mexico City wear their finest clothes at a fiesta held on Independence Day (September 16). Celebrations start the night before.

The huge Azteca Stadium in
Mexico City can hold 100,000 people.
Soccer, which is called futbol in
Mexico, is the most popular sport. In
Mexico, soccer clubs play in leagues.

Bullfights at Tijuana attract both Mexicans and Americans. Tijuana is on the United States frontier, near California. Spain introduced bull fighting into Mexico.

Indian artists are proud of their country's past. They keep alive styles that Indians used in ancient times, as shown by these masks.

December 12 is the Day of Our
Lady of Guadalupe, Mexico's
patron Saint. Parades are held
throughout Mexico. Indians often
wear glittering traditional costumes.

The farmlands of the fertile central Valley of Mexico contain many small Roman Catholic churches. Most Mexicans are Roman Catholics. The snow-capped mountain behind the church is a volcano named Ixtacihuatl.

This nativity play is being performed in the Shrine of the Virgin of the Remedies, Patroness of the Spaniards. Prayers are offered to her for rain and cures for sickness. Spanish missionaries brought Christianity to Mexico. Christian feast-days, or fiestas, are common.

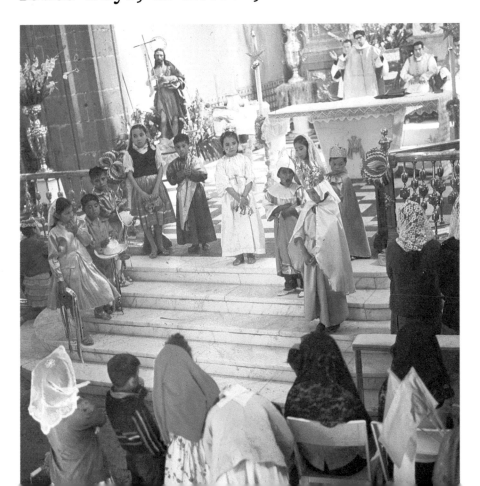

Guadalajara is Mexico's second largest city. It also has many lovely Spanish buildings and is popular with tourists.

Tourism brings in much needed
money for Mexico. Acapulco and
its superb beaches attract people from
all over the world, especially America.

Index